THE
OFFICIAL
FABLEHAVEN
COOKBOOK

Wondrous Recipes Inspired by the Characters from the Series

THE
OFFICIAL
FABLEHAVEN
COOKBOOK

Wondrous Recipes Inspired by the Characters from the Series

BRANDON MULL
& CHERIE MULL

SHADOW
MOUNTAIN
PUBLISHING

To Pam, Marjorie, and Gladys—
thanks for preparing countless meals
and treats over the years.—Brandon

For Bryson, Davis, Lila, Breck, and Grace.
Good food is always better
when shared with those we love.

Also for Grandma Susie,
who sparked my love of baking.
And my mother, who showed me
there is magic in the world.—Cherie

Illustrations by Brandon Dorman
Miscellaneous backgrounds and images provided by Garth Bruner, Adobe Stock Images, and Getty Images

Photographs and recipes © 2023 Cherie Mull
"The Missing Brownies: A Fablehaven Adventure" © 2023 Creative Concepts, LC

Visit us at shadowmountain.com

Library of Congress Cataloging-in-Publication Data
CIP on file
ISBN 978-1-63993-089-0

Printed in China
RR Donnelley, Dongguan, China

10 9 8 7 6 5 4 3 2 1

CONTENTS

The MISSING BROWNIES

Wearing the shorts and T-shirt he had slept in, Knox raced into Grandma Sorenson's kitchen in the main house at Fablehaven, socks slipping on the hardwood floor, his sister Tess a few paces behind him. When conducting culinary experiments with the magical creatures called brownies, morning was the time to check the results.

Knox had left out marshmallows, graham crackers, and chocolate bars on the counter, wondering if the brownies would do the obvious and make s'mores, or if they would produce something more inventive. In another cluster on the side counter, Tess had laid out crunchy peanut butter, honeycombs from the apiary, white flour, sugar, salt, vegetable oil, and yeast. She was hoping for peanut butter and honey on fresh, homemade bread.

It was difficult to anticipate how the brownies would combine ingredients. Knox had discovered that if he left instructions, they were disregarded. The more ingredients he provided, the less certain the outcome. Further complicating predictability, the little creatures had access to a dedicated brownie pantry stocked with spices and other sundries they could use to enhance whatever material was left out for their use.

The previous night, Knox had tried something new. He had printed out a couple of math assignments from the previous school year. Leaving a sharpened pencil beside the worksheets, Knox hoped to get the answer to one of his most burning questions—would brownies finish your homework?

Sliding to a stop beside the counter, Knox found all the ingredients gone and two pies in their place. Tess arrived beside him. "Are those your pies or mine?"

Knox looked around at the otherwise empty countertops. "They must have combined all our ingredients to make them."

"No s'mores?" Tess asked. "No PB&H?"

"The brownies like to do their own thing," Knox said. "That's what makes them interesting."

"That has long been true of their kind," Grandma Sorenson said, entering the kitchen. "You can count on brownies to make *something*. But it's difficult to guess the exact outcome. Over time I've noticed they have some favorite combinations, which is the only pattern I have found."

"What about your homework?" Tess asked, crossing to the table. Then she laughed.

"What?" Knox asked.

"Come see."

Knox turned toward the table and found his two worksheets folded into paper airplanes. The pencil had been used to add markings to the aircraft. He picked up one and threw it. The paper airplane flew straight and true before swooping into a landing and sliding into the wall. Knox unfolded the other airplane. Not a single math question had been answered.

"So much for living the good life," Knox said.

"Shall I cut the pie?" Grandma asked.

"If it means pie for breakfast, absolutely," Tess replied.

Grandma carved out a triangular piece and set it on a plate. She eyed the slice and sniffed it. "Chocolate, peanut butter, and marshmallow, sweetened mostly with honey, I believe. You may have one piece with breakfast."

"Thank you," Tess said.

"The brownies do this every night?" Knox asked. "No holidays?"

"If ingredients are made available," Grandma said. "Or if something needs mending. I make sure to leave out projects regularly."

"What do they get in return?" Knox asked.

Grandma folded her arms and cocked her head. "The joy of being useful and creative, I suppose."

"They also get twenty percent of anything they produce from raw ingredients," Grandpa Sorenson said, coming into the room wearing a plaid shirt, jeans, and work boots.

"But the pies aren't missing any ingredients," Knox observed.

"They're more skillful than that," Grandpa said. "Rest assured they made a third, smaller pie for themselves. It's fortuitous you've taken an interest in the brownies."

"Why?" Knox asked.

"We have a visitor," Grandpa said.

"Is it a brownie?" Tess enthused. "I've never seen one during the day. And they scatter when I try to watch them at night."

"Brownies cherish their privacy," Grandpa said. "Though they're nocturnal, they do make appearances during the day, much as we can go out at night, when it suits us. If you're willing to put breakfast on hold, you should join me in my office."

Knox took a hurried bite of pie. The sweet blend of chocolate, peanut butter, and marshmallow tempted him to linger, but as Tess hurried with Grandpa to his office, Knox followed behind. Knox passed through the dark wooden pocket doors, ignoring the memorabilia on the walls and the knick-knacks atop the desk. His attention locked onto the tiny guest seated in one of the high-backed leather armchairs. The brownie seemed extra small on the large chair. He wore a gray tunic, clean sandals, and a hat that looked like leaves stitched together. The brownie tilted his wrinkled face at Knox, then looked to Grandpa.

"Who are these two?" the brownie asked in a chirping voice.

"Garus, I would like you to meet my grandson, Knox, and my grand-daughter, Tess," Grandpa said. "Kids, this is Garus, son of Gimble, of the woodland brownies."

Scowling, the brownie stood up on his chair, less than a foot tall, one fist on his little hip. "I came here for *help*, not to meet the family."

"You look different than the other brownies," Tess said. "Wilder."

"Unlike the brownies you have encountered, Garus is not associated with a household," Grandpa explained. "His people live in the forest."

"At least he wears clothes," Knox said. "Doesn't look like he showers much."

"I dress to match the occasion!" Garus exclaimed, sputtering. He straightened his tunic. "Why would I follow every human convention? Stan, this is an emergency."

"Please explain the situation," Stan said. "My grandchildren have more experience with magical creatures than you might expect."

Garus folded his wiry arms. "I didn't trek all this way for help from your distant relations. Rather, my people are appealing to the caretaker to remedy the situation directly."

"As caretaker, this is part of my remedy," Grandpa said.

"Is that hat made of actual leaves?" Knox asked, leaning close.

Garus wrinkled his forehead. "Felt, kiddo. Leaves would rot and fall apart."

"Not if you used magic," Tess said.

The brownie raised an eyebrow. "I'll live ten lifetimes before I use magic to make leaves stay ever fresh for the sake of headwear."

"Your predicament," Grandpa prompted.

Garus eyed the three of them. "All right. I suppose this is what I get for interacting with humans." He sighed before continuing, head bowed. "A monster is abducting brownies from our community."

"Oh, no!" Tess cried. "What kind of monster?"

"We're not sure," the brownie said. "It's a wily brute. None who have seen the creature remain with us."

"Because they're dead?" Knox asked.

Garus shook his head. "Nay. Had they perished, I would have felt their deaths." He placed a hand over his heart. "The missing brownies have been taken alive, sure as I'm standing here."

"How many?" Tess asked.

"Five brownies have been lost," Garus said. "The abductions happened on three separate nights."

Knox frowned. "Have you taken measures to—"

"Of course we've taken measures," Garus interrupted. "Brownies are notoriously difficult to spot. Let alone nab. Especially those of us who dwell in the wilderness. Have you ever seen a wild brownie at Fablehaven?"

"Not until now," Knox said.

"As expected," Garus said. "We'd hear you coming a mile off and hide long before you drew near. Do brownies go missing from time to time? Sure. Life is dangerous. But it's a rarity. That first night when two brownies vanished, our community went into high alert. Yet after taking every precaution, three more were taken." Garus shook his head. "This monstrosity is like nothing we've ever known." He straightened. "I stand here as envoy to solicit protection for my kind."

Grandpa knelt down. "I'm very sorry for your losses," he said. "I'm troubled by this tragedy, and I agree the perpetrator must be brought to justice. Knox, Tess, will you investigate and report back to me?"

"Really?" Knox asked. "Sure. Yes. Absolutely!"

"The grandkids?" Garus cried, clutching the sides of his head. "We're facing our greatest enemy of the past century, and he lends us his grandkids?"

"I have held this office for a long time," Grandpa said. "I harbor my own suspicions that I wish to explore. Meanwhile Knox and Tess can gather information. These children have accomplished much. They may be young, but they are not novices. I won't live forever, and I want them to learn to watch over the preserve."

"Let them practice on the fairies," Garus pleaded. "Loan them out to the gnomes. We cannot lose more of our people."

Tess looked up at Grandpa. "Maybe you should make sure they get the help they need."

"I am," Grandpa said. "You and your brother are perfectly capable. Take Hugo. Garus will lead you to his settlement."

The brownie brightened. "They'll have the golem?"

"Yes," Grandpa said.

Garus slapped his knee. "Why didn't you tell me that at first? The golem is who I was hoping for all along . . . no disrespect intended."

"None taken," Grandpa said, spreading his hands. "When it comes to catching monsters, Hugo is my superior in many regards."

The brownie hopped nimbly to the floor and waved an arm. "Let's go. We're wasting time."

"What exactly should we do?" Knox asked Grandpa.

"Investigate," Grandpa said. "Learn the identity of the abductor. Then we'll bring the culprit to justice."

"What if the monster tries to capture us?" Tess asked.

"Have Hugo restrain him," Grandpa said. "Off you go. I have my own hunches to investigate."

Rays of morning sunlight slanted down through the trees. Summer dew beaded on leaves and long blades of grass. Hugo plodded along, mossy feet thumping against the faint trail, supporting Tess in one earthen hand and holding Knox with the other. Garus perched atop the golem's head. More than eight feet tall, Hugo was a humanoid with apelike proportions formed entirely from soil and stone. As the golem advanced through the silent forest, his body made little creaks and groans of the type that might precede a cave-in.

Knox had not been to this eastern part of Fablehaven. He gazed in fascination at human-sized marble statues crawling with ivy, faces worn away by time. When outside the yard at Fablehaven, Knox had usually been with an adult—or at least somebody experienced, like Seth or Kendra. But since his cousins were on an errand at Wyrmroost, the closest thing they had to a seasoned adventurer was Hugo.

"Did your people make those statues?" Tess asked.

"Not our style," Garus replied. "Those were the work of a gorgon. Don't fret—she's long gone."

"The statues are people who turned to stone?" Knox asked.

"Some folks gather petrified wood," Garus said. "Gorgons collect petrified people."

"Maybe a gorgon took your friends," Tess suggested.

"We'd have heard whispers if such a powerful menace were abroad," Garus said. "But I won't rule anything out."

Hugo turned from the scant trail, wading through bushes. He raised and lowered Knox and Tess to help them avoid branches. After ducking under the heavy bough of a massive oak, Hugo set them down, while Garus climbed expertly down the golem and dropped to the ground.

They had reached a clearing edged with elms, their branches fanning out wide. A little creek flowed across the far side of the meadow. Knox noticed several small waterwheels turning with the flow of the current. A variety of windmills protruded from tree trunks and others topped the larger branches. Spindly blades with sails of colorful fabric rotated in the gentle breeze, some as small as dinner plates, the largest nearly the diameter of a bicycle wheel.

"I like the carvings on the sides of the waterwheels," Tess said.

Giving a little nod, Garus surveyed the meadow. "We blend our workmanship with the surroundings. Devices can be functional while also pleasing the eye."

"Where were the brownies when they were taken?" Knox asked.

"Not indoors or below ground, if that's your meaning," Garus said. "Happened out in the open. All three incidents occurred in the evening."

"Witnesses?" Hugo asked in a deep voice like weighty stones grinding together.

Garus shook his head. "Nobody saw what happened. That's the problem."

"Were there any clues?" Tess asked. "Signs of a scuffle?"

A little voice chirped gibberish from a nearby bush. Knox saw the face of a female brownie peeking out.

"What's she saying?" Knox whispered.

"She's reminding him about acorns," Tess said.

Garus glanced her way. "You speak Rowian?"

"I spend lots of time with fairies," Tess said.

Garus gave an impressed nod. "Aye," he said, turning back to the female brownie in the bush and flicking the side of his own head. "We found Dalia's basket of acorns over yonder. And we located one of Timmet's shoes some distance beyond our borders."

"Show us," Hugo said.

"Four acorns and the shoe have already been collected," Garus said. "Waste not, want not. But I can show you where we found them."

Hugo nodded and Garus led them out of the meadow and over to a patch of wild raspberries higher up the stream. The brownie moved in quick, squirrel-like bursts, forcing Knox and Tess to hurry if they wanted to keep up. Knox noticed a few squat houses that looked like fat, brown mushrooms with round windows. Woodsmoke drifted up from vertical pipes in the shingled roofs, and miniature weather vanes swiveled in the breeze. He also observed more waterwheels and windmills.

"We don't typically invite outsiders into our community," Garus said. "The other brownies are aware of your presence but remain hidden. Take no offense. We prefer to be left alone."

"It's a beautiful town," Tess said.

"The best of it is underground," Garus said. "It's inaccessible for folks your size."

"I wish I could shrink down and see it," Tess said.

"It's safer to keep outsiders away from our secrets," Garus replied. "Please keep our location private."

"We will," Knox assured him. "We're caretakers in training."

Hugo lunged forward, crouched, and pressed a thick finger to the ground. "Acorns."

"Yes," Garus said, sounding surprised. "That's right where we found the basket. A couple of acorns had spilled out."

Hugo extended his large, stony hands and moved them palms downward over the ground, skimming the turf between the raspberry bushes. "Two taken here," Hugo said.

"Exactly right," Garus confirmed.

"Where find shoe?" Hugo asked.

"I'll wager Timmet dropped it deliberately," Garus said. "He would not have wandered so far outside our boundaries. But he is clever enough to leave a trail if he were taken."

"What about the other shoe?" Knox asked. "If he was leaving a trail, he had two."

"We only found the one," Garus said. He stroked his lips. "Could be an opportunity." He raised his voice. "Dunwick! Bring the shoe." Then he looked up at Hugo. "This way."

Garus led them away from the stream, nimbly weaving through dense undergrowth. Hugo picked up Knox and Tess, then pushed through the briars and other vegetation with ease. They reached a gentle slope dominated by shagbark hickory, towering trees with long strips of overlapping bark curving outward. Hugo put Knox and Tess down gently.

"Here," Garus said, pointing at a spot on the ground.

Pivoting at the waist, Hugo waved his palms around. He moved several steps up the slope, then squatted down and indicated an indentation in a soft patch of dirt.

"Tracks?" Garus asked.

"What kind of tracks?" Tess asked, craning to see.

"Ogre?" Knox guessed. "Werewolf?"

"Satyr," Hugo said.

"I have the shoe," a shrill voice cried. A tiny young man came racing from the direction of the stream, a green shoe in his hands. It was much more stylish than the sandals Garus wore. The youth sported black trousers, a crimson shirt, and an embroidered vest.

Hugo held out his hand and the young brownie placed the shoe in it. Hugo pinched the footwear between his thumb and forefinger, pondered it for a moment, then handed it back. "Come," the golem said, placing Garus back atop his head. He scooped up Knox and Tess.

"Tell Carla I'll be back before long," Garus called.

Hugo ran with long, loping strides. Knox squinted his eyes at the wind in his face as they swished through foliage and dodged between trees. He doubted whether a horse could gallop much faster.

"Do you know where you're going, Hugo?" Tess called.

"Yes," the golem replied.

"I think we're heading back toward the house," Knox said.

"Almost," Hugo rumbled.

"Golems have different perceptions than you and I," Garus explained. "There are no eyes inside those hollows in his head. He has no ears. A being doesn't need to see and hear if it can simply *sense* things."

Hugo pounded along, eventually coming to a stop outside a cozy house.

"Wait," Knox said. "This is where Newel and Doren live!"

Hugo crouched and picked up a second tiny shoe.

"Oh, no," Tess said. "We better get Grandpa."

Grandpa walked with quick, determined strides, his work boots leaving distinct footprints in the soil. Knox and Tess had to occasionally jog to keep up. Hugo lumbered behind them, Garus perched on his rocky shoulder.

Grandpa had listened quietly when Knox explained how the trail had led to Newel and Doren's house. At the end of the report, Grandpa gave a stiff nod, then apologized to Garus, assuring him that the abducted brownies were almost certainly unharmed. Eyes intense, posture unusually erect, Grandpa had said little else as he led the group to Newel and Doren's cottage.

The simple home had several nice touches, including freshly painted trim, green shutters on the windows, and a welcome mat out front. Grandpa rapped three times on the sturdy front door. A moment later Doren opened up, his smile faltering a bit as he saw Hugo, then his eyes briefly widening when he noticed Garus.

"Hello, Stan," Doren said. "How may I help you?"

"Let's talk inside," Grandpa said. "Knox, Tess, come with me so you can explain. Hugo, stay with Garus. Don't let anyone come or go."

Doren stepped back from the door, admitting Stan and his grandkids. Newel came bounding over from where he had been watching TV, a mug of root beer in one hand. "Stan, Knox, Tess, what a pleasant surprise!" he said enthusiastically.

Doren pantomimed something to Newel, but stopped when Grandpa glared at him. "I wish this were a social call," Grandpa said.

"Me too, so you could join our detective movie marathon," Newel said.

"I've had a complaint from Garus of the woodland brownies," Grandpa said.

Newel looked confused. "Brownies in the woods? What kind? Chocolate fudge? Maple pecan?"

"I think they know," Doren said, shooting Newel a nervous glance.

Newel sighed in exasperation. "You can at least put on a bit of an act! No need to sell the farm at the first inquiry."

"Five brownies have been abducted," Knox said. "We followed a trail to your house. One of the brownies dropped his shoes."

"Circumstantial evidence," Newel said. "No judge worth his gavel would issue a warrant."

"We've been watching legal shows," Doren confided.

"You're on private property and I'm the landlord," Grandpa said. "I'll have Hugo search the premises."

Newel paused. "We're keeping them downstairs. They've been so ornery!"

"Won't even cook popcorn," Doren said.

"What do you expect?" Grandpa asked. "You abducted them!"

Newel held up a finger. "We relocated them so they could hone their professional skills. Brownies in the wild are a waste of aptitude."

Doren looked at the floor, shamefaced. "We wanted a taste of the good life."

"He wouldn't understand," Newel said to his friend. "Stan's got more brownies than a minotaur has fleas."

"The brownies at the house entered into a voluntary arrangement with the caretaker ages ago," Grandpa said. "It's a long-standing, mutually beneficial relationship."

"We wanted to start one of those," Doren said.

"I think you're supposed to *ask*," Knox said.

"The whole woodland brownie community is really upset," Tess said.

"Would you want to do favors for your kidnappers?" Knox asked.

"Maybe," Newel said. "If they were charming and had really hairy legs."

"What were you hoping the brownies would do?" Knox asked.

Doren shrugged. "Cook for us, clean, help expand our wardrobe."

"And we have some treasure," Newel admitted. "Imagine if they combined treasure inventively to create more valuable items."

"Like what?" Tess asked.

Doren rubbed his hands together. "Maybe mix gold, rubies, and emeralds to make a golden cat with ruby eyes and an emerald collar. Or a gilded bust of Newel."

Newel placed a hand over his heart. "Or a likeness of my dear departed mother."

"You can stop gunning for sympathy points," Grandpa said. "We have a diplomatic crisis on our hands."

"We'll promise to ask next time," Newel suggested. "No more taking unwary brownies."

Grandpa shook his head. "Good luck with that. I need you to do more than pledge better behavior in the future."

"How did you catch them?" Knox asked. "Brownies are hard to surprise."

"Outfoxing foxes is what we do," Newel said. "The details are a trade secret."

Grandpa glared.

"These are friends," Doren said. "Maybe we should tell them."

"Like with fishing, the secret is using the right bait," Newel said. "Research and experimentation have shown that brownies cannot resist pumpkin choco-late chip cupcakes."

"Spread a net, add leaves, then bait the trap with a cupcake," Doren said. "Freshly baked works best. Brownies are very discriminating."

"Lay the trap toward the edge of their community just before sundown," Newel said. "Most brownies are still sleeping. Only the earliest risers are out and about."

"That's terrible," Tess said. "Brownies aren't *fish*. They're little people. They have families."

"We need to make it right," Doren said, pounding a fist into his palm. "I know—the brownies can bring *us* ingredients, and we'll combine them in surprising ways."

"You're getting warmer," Grandpa said. "Tess, how can they make repara-tions?"

"An apology," Tess said. "First to those you took, then to Garus, then to the woodland brownie community."

"That's *three* apologies," Newel pointed out. "It sounds humiliating. How about a counteroffer? I buy an apologetic greeting card, and Doren can sign it. Show it to all the brownies you like."

"Not good enough," Knox said. "It has to be sincere and in person. *And* you should repay them."

"How?" Doren asked.

Tess and Knox looked at each other.

"Give a piece of treasure to each brownie you abducted," Knox said.

Doren slapped a hand to his forehead. "That's *five* items of treasure!"

"Copper coins," Newel said out of the side of his mouth.

"If you go with coins, they have to be silver at least," Knox said. "Nothing worth less than that is acceptable."

"The brownies are so small," Tess said. "Didn't you learn anything from how the giants treated you?"

"Sure," Newel said. "It's better to be the giant."

"He's got a point," Doren agreed.

"You should have learned it's not fair to pick on little guys," Tess scolded.

"Hey, we stopped picking on the nipsies," Newel said.

"They were the littlest guys," Doren added.

"Stan, these kids are intoxicated with power," Newel said. "Please give us a more reasonable way out of this nightmare."

"My way would be markedly more severe," Grandpa said heavily. "I would enact all that the kids have recommended, plus I would also take away electricity for a time . . . including television privileges."

Newel blanched, then swayed toward Doren, who steadied him. They huddled together to confer. Newel made some pointed gestures. Doren shook his head and jabbed his finger against Newel's chest.

"Fine," Newel said, facing Grandpa. "We accept the terms established by Knox and Tess. We'll apologize and make reparations."

"We're sorry, Stan," Doren said. "It seemed like such a brilliant idea. I mean, we thought the brownies enjoyed making things."

"They do," Grandpa said. "When they're treated with respect."

"Well, good riddance to the lot downstairs," Newel said. "All they make is insults."

"Several of which stung," Doren added.

"You should begin by apologizing to the prisoners," Tess said. "Then Garus."

"I wouldn't mind hearing Newel apologize to Grandpa as well," Knox said.

"That's *four*," Newel muttered. After a quick glance at the television, he cleared his throat. "Stan, I let you down, and I mistreated innocent brownies. Fablehaven deserves better. I'm sorry for my part in Doren's plot."

"It was your idea," Doren grumbled.

"We both ignored the most important rule when capturing a brownie," Newel said.

"What's that?" Knox asked.

"Don't get caught," Doren said. "And we forgot one more thing—don't bring home a wild creature unless you know how to tame it."

"I just hope Garus and his people will forgive you," Grandpa said. "I've seen what brownies can do when they become truly angry. They make much better allies than enemies."

Doren scratched his chin. "Newel, I think we should make enough pumpkin chocolate chip cupcakes for all the woodland brownies."

Newel sighed and nodded. "From now on, we'll protect them. May Doren and I be the worst monsters they ever face."

Pumpkin Chocolate Chip Cupcakes

HAVE YOU EVER WONDERED whether brownies live in your home? One way to find out is to leave a Pumpkin Chocolate Chip Cupcake on the counter overnight. If it's gone the next morning, you likely have small, magical creatures dwelling in your walls or dungeon. Please use this treat responsibly. Sure, you could try to capture a brownie, but why risk retribution from the magical community?

1 (15.25-ounce) package spice cake mix

⅓ cup all-purpose flour

1 (3-ounce) package vanilla pudding

4 eggs at room temperature

1 cup canned pumpkin puree, approximately ½ (15-ounce) can

¾ cup sour cream at room temperature

⅓ cup canola oil

¾ cup water

1½ cups chocolate chips

1 batch of cream cheese frosting (see recipe for Grandma Larsen's cream cheese frosting on page 72), divided

1 (.67-ounce) tube red gel food coloring

1 (.67-ounce) tube yellow gel food coloring

1 (4.25-ounce) tube black decorating icing, or black jellybeans and/or candy corn, for jack-o'-lantern faces

1. Preheat oven to 350 degrees F. Line muffin tins with cupcake wrappers (approximately 24 to 30 cupcakes).

2. Combine cake mix, flour, pudding, eggs, canned pumpkin, sour cream, oil, and water in a large mixer bowl or stand mixer. Beat at low speed until moistened. Beat at medium speed for about 2 minutes, scraping down sides of bowl. Stir in chocolate chips.

3. Pour into lined cupcake pans, filling about ½ to ⅔ full.

4. Bake for approximately 15-20 minutes, or until toothpick inserted into center of cupcake comes out clean. You can also check cupcakes by gently pressing a finger onto the top of a cupcake. If it pops back up, cupcakes are done. If it sinks, continue to cook for a few more minutes.

5. Move cupcakes to cooling rack to cool completely.

6. Use gel food coloring to tint the frosting orange, 1 cup at a time. Frost the cupcakes with the orange frosting, then use the tube of black decorating icing or candy to make jack-o'-lantern faces.

BREAKFAST

Apple Pancakes

SATURDAY MORNING PANCAKES ARE a Sorenson family tradition. Apple pancakes dusted with powdered sugar are Kendra's favorite.

2 tablespoons butter

½ teaspoon cinnamon

1½ tablespoons sugar

1½ apples, sliced thinly

2 eggs at room temperature

½ cup milk

½ cup flour

½ teaspoon salt

2 tablespoons melted butter

Powdered sugar

1. Preheat oven to 400 degrees F.

2. Melt 2 tablespoons butter over medium heat in an oven-safe frying pan or skillet. Add cinnamon and sugar and mix well. Add apple slices and cook until soft.

3. In a separate bowl, beat the eggs. Add the milk, flour, salt, and melted butter. Whisk together until well mixed. Pour the mixture into the pan over the cooked apples.

4. Bake for 25–30 minutes, until pancake rises and is golden brown.

5. Remove from oven and dust with powdered sugar.

6. Cut into slices and serve.

Sorenson Buttermilk Pancakes

"DON'T EAT MORE THAN you want," Grandma said. Kendra realized she had been toying with her pancakes, procrastinating the next bite. "I'm kind of tense," Kendra confessed, eating another forkful, hoping her face looked pleasant as she chewed. "I'll have hers," Seth offered, having almost finished his stack. "I'm not watching my figure for Gavin."

—Fablehaven, book 5: *Grip of the Shadow Plague*, p. 285

2 cups buttermilk at room temperature

2 eggs at room temperature

4 tablespoons butter, melted

2 cups flour

2 tablespoons sugar

2 teaspoons baking powder

1 teaspoon baking soda

1 teaspoon salt

⅛ to ¼ cup milk

1. Mix buttermilk, eggs, and melted butter together.

2. Add dry ingredients and whisk until mixed.

3. Add milk slowly until the batter can be poured easily.

4. Heat skillet to 325 degrees F.

5. Use approximately ¼ cup batter per pancake. Cook until pancakes are a light golden brown on both sides and the center is cooked through.

Sorenson Buttermilk Syrup

1 cup sugar

¾ cup buttermilk

½ cup butter

2 tablespoons corn syrup

1 teaspoon baking soda

2 teaspoons vanilla

1. Bring all ingredients except vanilla to a boil in a large saucepan. Reduce heat and simmer for 7 minutes. Remove from heat. Add vanilla and let cool. Leftover syrup can be refrigerated for later use.

SECRET SATYR SOFT GRANOLA

PERFORMING MISCHIEF REQUIRES A lot of energy. This closely guarded recipe was donated by Newel and Doren. In return, they have asked for one battery from every person who eats this delicious soft granola.

2¼ cups rolled oats

¼ cup ground flaxseed

⅓ cup powdered milk

½ cup shredded coconut (sweetened or unsweetened)

½ cup chopped pecans (can substitute almonds or other nuts)

1½ tablespoons chia seeds

½ teaspoon kosher salt

⅓ cup coconut oil, melted

½ cup raw honey, liquid/soft

1 teaspoon vanilla

1. Preheat oven to 350 degrees F. Combine all ingredients. Spread evenly on baking sheet. Bake 10 minutes. Allow to cool, then transfer to airtight container.

Maddox's Yogurt Parfaits

THIS RECIPE ORIGINATED DURING a trip Maddox took to France to visit a fairy broker, where he was served this sweet and creamy parfait. Maddox threw in a rose-tinted dune sprite so he could walk away with the recipe. He has since found that the confection also works as fairy bait.

4 cups vanilla, strawberry, or Greek yogurt

1 cup Secret Satyr Soft Granola (see recipe on page 22)

1 cup chopped strawberries

½ cup blueberries

½ cup raspberries

1. Layer ½ cup yogurt in 4 clear cups or small mason jars. Sprinkle a handful of granola. Top with a few spoonfuls of strawberries and a handful of blueberries and raspberries. Repeat layers one more time. Eat immediately or refrigerate and serve later.

Knox's Favorite Berry & Honey Oatmeal

LENA WOULD PREPARE THIS concoction for Patton after long nights chasing down goblins, to nourish his belly and calm his nerves. It became a tradition for subsequent generations. Knox was dubious about the dish at first, but it grew into his most requested breakfast.

"Delicious. The berries sweeten it to perfection."—Tess

"That was the best oatmeal I've ever had. It usually tastes like mud."—Knox

1 cup quick cooking oats

1 cup frozen mixed berries

1 tablespoon honey

1 tablespoon brown sugar, divided

2 tablespoons heavy cream or milk

1. Cook the oats according to package directions. In a separate saucepan, combine the berries and honey. Cook on medium heat for about 3–5 minutes until the berries release their juices. Remove from heat.

2. Divide the oatmeal into two bowls. Pour half the berry mixture into each bowl of oatmeal. Top with 1½ teaspoons brown sugar and drizzle with cream or milk. Stir and enjoy.

Grandma Sorenson's Egg in a Hole

NOBODY IS CERTAIN WHY Grandma Sorenson likes to make this recipe, but many in the family suspect it could be linked to her time as a chicken.

Nonstick cooking spray

1 slice of bread

1 tablespoon butter, softened

1 egg

Salt and pepper to taste

1. Heat a skillet or frying pan over medium-low heat. Spray with cooking spray. Using a cookie cutter or a knife, cut a 2-inch hole in the center of a bread slice, and discard the extracted piece. Butter both sides of the remaining slice of bread. Place the bread slice on the hot skillet. Crack an egg into the hole in the bread. Season with salt and pepper. Cook until the egg is beginning to firm up. Flip the bread and egg over and cook for about another minute, or until the egg white is completely cooked. Serve immediately.

Lena's Loaded Crepes

LENA WENT ON MANY adventures after her beloved Patton passed away. Working as a pastry chef in France expanded her culinary talents. February 2 is *le jour des crêpes* (the day of crepes) in France. *Bon appétit!*

---

2 cups milk (preferably whole or 2 percent milk)

1½ cups flour

4 large eggs at room temperature

3 tablespoons melted butter

1½ tablespoons sugar

½ teaspoon salt

1 teaspoon vanilla

Softened butter or nonstick cooking spray

Berries, bananas, cookie butter, Nutella, whipped topping, or Viola's Sweetened Whipped Cream (see page 60) for topping

1. Combine milk, flour, eggs, melted butter, sugar, salt, and vanilla in a blender until batter is smooth, about 30–60 seconds. Cover and refrigerate batter for at least 30 minutes.

2. Heat a frying pan (8-inch or larger) over medium-low heat. Spray with cooking spray or use a small amount of butter to grease pan. Pour about ¼ cup batter into the pan and swirl pan to form an even circle of batter.

3. Cook for about 1 minute, flip, and cook for about 1 more minute, until both sides are golden brown.

4. Serve with berries, bananas, cookie butter, Nutella, whipped cream, or other desired toppings.

Fairy Toast

THIS RECIPE ORIGINATED WITH a former caretaker at the Obsidian Waste preserve in Australia, who won't confirm if fairy magic was used in the creation of this tasty treat. What do you think?

2 slices of bread
Softened butter
Small sprinkles

1. For the simplest of magical treats, toast 2 pieces of bread. Spread with softened butter (or substitute biscoff cookie butter or Nutella), and cover with your favorite sprinkles or sanding sugar.

LUNCH
AND
SNACKS

Seth's PB&J Creations

SETH THINKS PEANUT BUTTER goes with just about anything. Do you have a favorite combination for Seth to try? Tell us about it at info@shadowmountain.com.

Sliced bread
Peanut butter

Optional Spreads/Toppings

Jam

Nutella

Banana, sliced

Marshmallow fluff

Cereal

Potato chips

 An easy way to make a peanut butter and jelly sandwich more exciting is to grill it! Butter the outside of the bread and cook it on a skillet over medium-low heat until golden brown, or place in a panini press until hot. Even better with home-made jam!

Or, try peanut butter and Nutella. Add sliced bananas and enjoy!

Another great combo is peanut butter and marshmallow fluff. Banana slices are optional on this one as well.

Cereal lovers may want to add a handful of your favorite cereal to your PB&J for a crunchy surprise!

Another way to add some crunchy texture and a hint of salt is to put a handful of potato chips in the middle.

OGRE STEW

WARNING: THE AROMA OF this scrumptious stew can travel for miles and has been known to attract ogres and trolls. It is strongly recommended that you close your windows when simmering and serving this stew or you may have very large unexpected guests for dinner.

1 pound chicken breast, cubed

1 medium onion, diced

1½ teaspoons garlic powder

1 tablespoon oil

2 (19-ounce) cans white beans, drained

2 (4-ounce) cans of diced mild green chilis

1 (14.5-ounce) can chicken broth

1 teaspoon salt

1 teaspoon ground cumin

½ teaspoon black pepper

1 teaspoon oregano

¼ teaspoon cayenne pepper

1 cup sour cream

½ cup whipping cream

1. Sauté chicken, onion, and garlic powder in oil until chicken is cooked through. Add beans, green chilis, chicken broth, and seasonings. Bring to a boil. Simmer uncovered for 30 minutes. Remove from heat. Stir in whipping cream and sour cream.

2. Serve with your choice of chopped green onion, fresh avocado, shredded cheese, tortilla chips, or other toppings.

Lost Mesa Corn Avocado Salsa

THIS SALSA ORIGINATING FROM the Lost Mesa preserve is well-known among humans in the magical community. Not only is the salsa fresh and flavorful, it is also rumored to repel zombies. Skeptical? The MCDC (Magical Center for Disease Control) has zero reports of a person killed by a zombie within forty-eight hours of consuming Lost Mesa Corn Avocado Salsa.

2 firm avocados, diced

½ red onion, diced

1 jalapeño pepper, ribs and seeds removed, finely diced

Juice of 1 lime

2 tomatoes, diced

Chopped cilantro to taste

Kosher salt to taste

1 tablespoon vinegar

1 teaspoon sugar

1. Combine all ingredients in a bowl and mix. Cover and refrigerate before serving. Serve the salsa with tortilla chips, grilled chicken, inside a taco, or as a salad topping.

DRAGON ROASTED PEPPERS WITH GOAT CHEESE

THIS RECIPE DATES BACK to Branderbrux the Bold*, a slayer who dispatched fourteen dragons. He and his dwarven legion turned a tragedy into a feast after a two-headed dragon scorched a herd of goats grazing in a pepper patch.

*As found in *Legend of the Dragon Slayer*, "Enumeration of Notable Dragon Slayers," p. 56

3-4 large sweet bell peppers (red, orange, or yellow), or 8-10 baby bell peppers

Olive oil

Crumbled goat cheese

Salt and pepper to taste

Oregano (optional)

Thyme (optional)

1. Preheat oven to 400 degrees F. Slice peppers and remove seeds. For large peppers, cut into 6-8 pieces. For baby peppers, cut in half. Drizzle or brush peppers with olive oil. Sprinkle goat cheese until lightly covered. Season with salt and pepper, other seasonings as desired.

2. Bake for about 15-20 minutes until cheese is golden brown and peppers are browned on the edges.

Easy Fair Folk Tortilla Pizzas

THE FAIR FOLK HAVE mastered the art of living sumptuously. Not wanting to trust outsiders with their more complex recipes, Lord Dargorel said, "Even the lowliest human should be able to manage this one."

1 package 10-inch flour tortillas

1 (24-ounce) jar marinara sauce

1 (16-ounce) bag shredded mozzarella cheese

1 (5-ounce) package pepperoni (full-size or mini)

1. Preheat oven to 350 degrees F. Place two tortillas on cookie sheet. Spoon desired amount of marinara sauce onto tortillas, and spread evenly. Cover with mozzarella cheese. Place pepperonis to make a smiley face. Bake for 5 minutes or until cheese is melted and lightly golden brown. Slice and serve.

MURIEL'S PRETZEL KNOTS

LIKE MAKING A WISH before blowing out birthday candles, go ahead and blow on a pretzel knot, then make a wish before eating. Remember, don't tell anyone your wish.

1½ cups lukewarm water	3 cups all-purpose flour
1¼ teaspoons active dry yeast	2 tablespoons baking soda
3 tablespoons brown sugar	2 cups warm water
1¼ teaspoons salt	4 tablespoons melted butter
1 cup bread flour	Coarse salt

1. Add yeast to warm water. Stir until dissolved. Add sugar and salt. Stir until dissolved. Add flour slowly. Knead dough or use dough hook on electric mixer to knead until dough is smooth and elastic.

2. Let the dough rise for 30–60 minutes until about doubled in size.

3. Preheat oven to 450 degrees F.

4. Mix 2 cups warm water with 2 tablespoons baking soda in a small bowl. Stir often.

5. Pinch off portions of risen dough and roll into ¼- to ½-inch-thick ropes. Tie into knot shapes.

6. Dip pretzels in soda solution and place on greased or lined baking sheet.

7. Bake for about 10 minutes until golden brown.

8. Remove from oven and brush with melted butter. Sprinkle with coarse salt.

Bubda's Sloppy Guac

LIFE GETS LONELY FOR a hermit troll. Bubda finds solace in this special recipe that he shares only with his closest friends.

3 large, ripe avocados

½ small red onion, diced finely

1 large or 2 small tomatoes, chopped

2–4 tablespoons fresh cilantro, chopped

½ jalapeño pepper, ribs and seeds removed, finely diced

2 garlic cloves, minced

Juice of 1 lime

Salt and pepper to taste

Cucumbers, sliced in coins

Olives, sliced

1. Slice avocados in half lengthwise. Remove pit, and scoop avocado into bowl. Mash with a fork to desired consistency. Add chopped vegetables, cilantro, garlic, and lime juice. Season with salt and pepper. Stir.

2. Use cucumbers and olives to make a hermit troll face. Serve with chips or veggies, or use as a topping for tacos.

Grunhold Garlic Hummus

THE CENTAURS OF GRUNHOLD are very private about their culinary dishes. Favoring Mediterranean fare, they require large quantities of food to satisfy multiple stomachs. Centaurs typically add extra garlic to the recipe to keep the flies away.

1 (15-ounce) can chickpeas, drained and rinsed

¼ cup fresh lemon juice

¼ cup tahini (see tahini recipe below)

1 garlic clove, minced

2 tablespoons olive oil

½ teaspoon ground cumin

½ teaspoon sea salt

2–4 tablespoons water

Salt and pepper to taste

1. Combine all ingredients except water in a food processor. Process until well blended. Scrape down sides of bowl and continue to process until smooth. Add additional salt and pepper to taste. Slowly add water until the consistency is smooth and creamy.

2. Serve with vegetables and pita.

Tahini

1 cup sesame seeds

2–4 tablespoons canola or olive oil

Pinch of salt

1. Toast sesame seeds in a large saucepan over medium-low heat, stirring constantly until seeds are very light golden (3–5 minutes). Watch carefully— seeds can burn quickly.

2. Transfer toasted seeds to a plate or tray to cool completely.

3. Place cooled seeds in a food processor and process for about 1 minute. Add oil and process for 2–3 minutes, scraping down the sides of bowl if necessary. Add extra oil if needed, until the consistency is smooth and fluid. Add salt to taste.

Tanu's Heartening Tomato Soup

NO ONE MAKES BETTER soup than a potion master who knows how to combine the best ingredients for the creamiest, most comforting tomato soup. Especially satisfying on the night preceding the Winter Solstice. Optional: Add one drop of courage potion per one cup of soup.

12 tomatoes, quartered

1 large onion, cut into chunks

3–4 garlic cloves, quartered

2 tablespoons olive oil

2 tablespoons fresh thyme

1 teaspoon salt

¼ teaspoon pepper

Fresh or dried oregano and
  rosemary to taste

15 fresh basil leaves

Shredded Parmesan cheese

1. Preheat oven to 400 degrees F.

2. Place tomatoes, onion, and garlic in a 9x13 pan or rimmed cookie sheet. Drizzle olive oil over vegetables. Sprinkle with thyme, salt, pepper, oregano, and rosemary. Toss to coat.

3. Bake for 30 minutes, stirring once halfway through cooking, or until vegetables are juicy and soft. Remove from oven and let cool slightly.

4. Scoop half the tomato mixture and half the basil leaves into a blender. Process until smooth. Pour the soup into bowls.

5. Repeat with second half of tomato mixture and basil leaves. Alternately, scoop all the tomato mixture and basil leaves into a large high-sided bowl or dutch oven and blend with an immersion blender, then ladle the soup into bowls.

6. Top with shredded Parmesan cheese and serve with grilled cheese sandwiches, croutons, or crusty bread.

Midsummer Strawberry Salsa
with Cinnamon Sugar Tortilla Chips | 48

Mummy Dogs | 51

Zombie Cake Eyeballs | 52

Jack-o'-Lantern Pumpkin Pie Bars | 55

Coulter's Caramel Apples | 56

Midsummer Strawberry Salsa with Cinnamon Sugar Tortilla Chips

"GRANDPA SAID A NIGHT is coming when all the creatures here will run wild."

"Midsummer Eve. The festival night."

"What's it like?"

"I'd better not say."

—Fablehaven, book 1: *Fablehaven*, pp. 115–16

A FAVORITE SUMMER RECIPE to celebrate with after surviving the chaos of Midsummer's Eve. However, to avoid having your garden strawberries trampled and stomped on by unsavory creatures, we strongly recommend that you harvest your ripe produce the day before.

2 crisp Granny Smith apples, peeled and diced small

2 firm pears, peeled and diced small

2–3 kiwis, scooped out and chopped into small pieces

1 pint strawberries, diced

⅓ cup brown sugar

½ cup sugar

1 teaspoon cinnamon

1 package 10-inch flour tortillas

¼ to ½ cup melted or softened butter

1. Mix chopped fruit and brown sugar in large mixing bowl. Store in refrigerator until ready to eat.

2. Preheat oven to 350 degrees F. Mix sugar and cinnamon in a small bowl. Place 2 tortillas on a large cookie sheet. Spread with thin layer of butter. Cover with cinnamon sugar mixture. Use knife or pizza cutter to cut tortillas into wedges or strips. Bake in single layer for 8–10 minutes until lightly golden brown and crispy.

3. Use cinnamon sugar tortilla chips to scoop strawberry salsa.

Mummy Dogs

A VIVIBLIX IS VAMPIRIC in nature and can temporarily reanimate the dead with a single bite. For example, if a mummy shambles toward you, it's probably being controlled by a viviblix. Note: If one of your mummy dogs comes to life, devour it quickly. If they all come to life, run!

1 (8-ounce) can refrigerated crescent rolls or crescent dough sheet

8 hot dogs

Ketchup

Mustard

1. Preheat oven to 375 degrees F.

2. If using crescent rolls, unroll dough. Separate at perforations to create 4 rectangles, sealing dough at the diagonal seams. If using a dough sheet, unroll dough and cut into 4 rectangles.

3. With a knife or pizza cutter, cut each rectangle into 8 long strips.

4. Wrap 4 pieces of dough around each hot dog to look like mummy bandages. Leave a space, about ½-inch thick, toward the top of each hot dog to make a "face" on the mummy.

5. Place on baking sheet and bake about 15 minutes, or until dough is light golden brown and hot dogs are hot.

6. Use ketchup or mustard to make eyes on the mummy face.

Zombie Cake Eyeballs

IF AFTER MAKING THIS recipe you hear spectral voices, there are only three possibilities: 1. Your sibling is playing a prank on you. 2. You're baking in a graveyard. 3. You're a shadow charmer. If you *are* a shadow charmer, try coaxing these Zombie Cake Eyeballs into serving you.

Favorite cake recipe or boxed cake mix

1½ cups buttercream frosting, divided (see recipe on page 61) or 1 (16-ounce) tub of prepared frosting, divided

1 (12-ounce) bag white chocolate candy melts or wafers

Lollipop or cake pop sticks

Dark brown M&M's candies

¼ (.67-ounce) tube green gel food coloring

¼ (.67-ounce) tube red gel food coloring

Floral foam

1. Make a batch of your favorite cake recipe, or prepare a boxed cake mix according to package instructions. Cool the cake, then crumble into a large mixing bowl.

2. Add 1 cup of buttercream frosting or other prepared frosting. Mix together until fully blended.

3. Set in refrigerator to cool for at least 30 minutes.

4. Once chilled, roll out small (approximately 1½-inch) balls of cake mixture and place on cookie sheet. Put cookie sheet back in the refrigerator to chill for at least 30 minutes.

5. While the cake balls are chilling, start melting the white chocolate pieces. Pour about half the bag of candy melts into a microwave-safe bowl. Microwave on half power in 1-minute increments until the chocolate is melted and smooth. Do not overheat.

6. Remove cake balls from the refrigerator. Dip the very end of the lollipop stick in the melted white chocolate and stick into center of a cake ball, then allow to set for a few minutes. Once secure, dip the cake ball on the stick into the melted chocolate. Fully cover, allowing the excess to drip off. Place the stick in the floral foam to allow the cake pop to set. Repeat for remaining cake balls. You may need to re-chill the cake balls partway through, and you may also need to melt more white chocolate.

7. Once the cake pops are set, mix ¼ cup buttercream frosting and ¼ tube of green gel food coloring to make green frosting—adjusting the food coloring amount to make the frosting either more or less vibrant. Mix ¼ cup buttercream frosting and red gel food coloring to make red frosting, adjusting food coloring amount to make the frosting either more or less vibrant. Use two piping bags or small sandwich bags with a hole cut in the corner to decorate the cake pops by piping a small (approximately ¾-inch) circle of green frosting in the center of each ball. Stick a dark chocolate M&M candy in the center of the green circle, then pipe red wavy lines around the cake pop to look like a bloodshot eye.

Jack-o'-Lantern Pumpkin Pie Bars

THE FABLEHAVEN GREENHOUSE GROWS pumpkins year-round: white, yellow, orange, red, and green of all sizes. Everyone knows the importance of inviting fairies inside jack-o'-lanterns on a Festival Night. Eating these bars may lend you added protection against nefarious monsters, plus they are fun and easy to make.

For this recipe, Grandpa Sorenson produces fresh pumpkin puree from his Fablehaven pumpkins and also incorporates walrus butter. No worries if you don't have a supply of walrus butter or access to a walrus. Standard butter from your local grocery store will also work. But don't skimp on Viola's Sweetened Whipped Cream, the perfect topping for this yummy dessert.

Softened butter or nonstick cooking spray

1 (13-ounce) can evaporated milk

3 eggs, beaten

2 teaspoons pumpkin pie spice

½ teaspoon salt

1 cup sugar

2 cups canned pumpkin puree, approximately 1 (15-ounce) can

1 (15.25-ounce) package yellow cake mix

⅔ cup cold butter, cubed

1 cup prepared whipped cream (see recipe for Viola's Sweetened Whipped Cream on page 60) or 1 (8-ounce) tub whipped topping

1. Preheat oven to 350 degrees F.

2. Grease a 9x13 baking dish with butter or spray with nonstick cooking spray.

3. In a bowl, mix the evaporated milk, eggs, pumpkin pie spice, salt, sugar, and canned pumpkin.

4. Pour into the 9x13 pan. Sprinkle dry cake mix over the top. Drop the small butter cubes evenly over the top of the cake mix.

5. Bake for 30–40 minutes.

6. Allow to cool and serve with whipped cream or whipped topping.

Coulter's Caramel Apples

WHENEVER COULTER VISITS, NEWEL and Doren set aside their laziness and eagerly gather apples from the Fablehaven orchards. They are wild for Coulter's caramel apples. But he doesn't let the satyrs help prepare them. Not after Newel drank all the corn syrup. Seriously, don't leave a satyr unsupervised around any kind of syrup.

8 cold, tart apples, such as Braeburn, McIntosh, or Jonathan varieties

8 (¼-inch) wooden dowels, craft sticks, or large skewers

1¾ cups heavy whipping cream

1 cup light corn syrup

2 cups packed light brown sugar

¼ cup unsalted butter

¾ teaspoon salt

1 teaspoon vanilla

Optional toppings: crushed Oreos, crushed pretzels, mini M&M's, other candies, or white chocolate wafers or chocolate chips for drizzling or dipping

1. Line a cookie sheet with a silicone mat (preferred) or wax paper.

2. Prep the apples by removing their stems and washing with water and dish soap or using a vinegar bath to remove the wax coating. Rinse well and dry completely. Insert a dowel, stick, or skewer about ¾ of the way into the top of each apple.

3. To make the caramel, combine the heavy cream, corn syrup, brown sugar, butter, and salt in a large saucepan over medium heat. Stir with a wooden spoon or silicone spatula until butter is melted. Using a candy thermometer, allow the mixture to boil until it reaches 235 to 240 degrees F. This step should take about 15–20 minutes, until caramel is a medium golden brown. Remove the caramel from heat and stir in vanilla until just mixed. Allow the caramel to cool for about 15 minutes or until slightly thickened.

4. Once the caramel has thickened, take one apple on a stick and carefully dip it into the warm caramel, coating it almost completely. Let excess caramel drip off, and use a knife or spatula to scrape off extra on the bottom of the apple. Set the apple on the prepared cookie sheet to cool. Repeat until all apples are coated with caramel.

5. If adding toppings, allow caramel to set for about 15 seconds, and add the dry toppings such as crushed Oreos, crushed pretzels, M&M's, or other candies. If dipping in or drizzling with melted chocolate or white chocolate, follow the melting instructions from the Zombie Cake Eyeballs recipe on page 52, and allow the caramel to set completely before dipping in chocolate or drizzling melted chocolate over the apple. Additional toppings may be added to the chocolate before dipping as well.

TREATS

Viola's Sweetened Whipped Cream

VIOLA, THE MILCH COW, is older than the Fablehaven preserve, which was founded in 1711. At that time, she was brought over from Europe by ship. Born from a pedigreed family of milch cows on a preserve in the Pyrenees Mountains, she was about 100 years old when she made the voyage, and was already larger than an elephant. She gains size each year. Even if you don't use enchanted milk, this recipe will always taste magical.

1 cup heavy whipping cream, chilled
¼ cup powdered sugar
1 teaspoon vanilla

1. If using a stand mixer, combine all ingredients in the bowl of the stand mixer. Use the whisk attachment and beat on high speed until stiff peaks form (approximately 3 minutes).

2. If using a hand mixer, combine all ingredients in a medium bowl. Using whisk or beater attachments, beat on high speed until stiff peaks form.

 Recipe can easily be doubled if needed.

Raxtus's Shiny Buttercream Frosting

DRAGON TASTES ARE NOT normally in alignment with what humans enjoy. After all, do any people salivate when thinking about gulping down a rhino, horn and all? But Raxtus is no typical dragon. His appreciation for sweets is evidenced by this delicious icing, which he has licked from his sparkly chops on multiple occasions.

1 cup (2 sticks) unsalted butter, softened

4 cups powdered sugar, sifted

½ teaspoon salt

1½ teaspoons vanilla

¼ cup heavy whipping cream

1. Cream the butter until softened. Add 2 cups of the powdered sugar, and mix at low speed until moistened. Add the salt and vanilla. Mix at low speed until incorporated, then beat at medium-high speed for about a minute. Slowly add remaining powdered sugar, beating at low speed until incorporated. Gradually add whipping cream. Increase speed to medium-high and beat for a few minutes, scraping down sides occasionally. Beat until fluffy and lightened in color.

Bracken's Unicorn Shakes

YOU DON'T NEED TO be a unicorn to enjoy these rich and creamy shakes. Rumor has it that Bracken made them for Kendra on their first official date.

Buttercream frosting (see recipe on page 61)

Unicorn horns

Sugar cones

White chocolate candy melts

Shakes

10 scoops vanilla ice cream

¾ cup chopped frozen strawberries

½ to 1 cup milk

Toppings

Colored candy, such as Sixlets or mini M&M's

Strawberry-flavored marshmallows

Cotton candy

Sprinkles

Viola's Sweetened Whipped Cream (see recipe on page 60)

1. Spread a generous layer of frosting around the outside upper rim of a glass. Press colorful candies into the frosting. Place the glass in the freezer to set for 10–15 minutes. Repeat for every glass (makes up to 2 large or 4 small shakes).

2. To make a unicorn horn, fill a microwave-safe bowl with white chocolate candy melts. Follow the package instructions to melt the chocolate. (Heat at reduced power in 1-minute increments, stirring in between.) Dip a cone in the melted chocolate and tap off the excess. Set the cone on a piece of wax paper and cover with sprinkles. Let cool and set. To set faster, place in refrigerator.

3. To make the milkshake, add milk, ice cream, and frozen berries to a blender. Blend until smooth and creamy. Pour the shake into the cold glasses. Top with whipped cream and/or a large chunk of cotton candy. Place the unicorn horn on top of the cotton candy. Add marshmallows or other toppings. Enjoy!

Grandma Sorenson's Apple Pie

GRANNY SMITH APPLES AND Grandma Sorenson have the same initials—G. S. Grandma Sorenson places these two letters made from extra pie dough on top of every apple pie before placing it in the oven. The baked monogram says it all.

Pie Crust

Makes two 9-inch crusts

2 cups flour

1 teaspoon salt

⅔ cup plus 2 tablespoons shortening

¼ cup cold water

1. Combine flour and salt. Using a pastry blender, add shortening until particles are the size of large peas. Sprinkle with water, one tablespoon at a time, mixing with a fork until the flour mixture is moistened. Form into two balls. Place the first ball on a lightly floured surface and roll into a circle about 1 inch larger than the pan. Fold in half and place in pie pan. Roll out the top crust and set aside.

Pie Filling

1 cup sugar

1 teaspoon cinnamon

7 cups Granny Smith apples, thinly sliced

1½ tablespoons cold butter, cut into small cubes

Vanilla ice cream, Viola's Sweetened Whipped Cream (see recipe on page 60), or whipped topping

1. Heat oven to 425 degrees F.

2. Mix sugar and cinnamon. Gently toss the apples with the cinnamon sugar mix. Heap the coated apples into the prepared crust in the pie pan. Dot with butter.

3. Cover with top crust. Seal the crust with your fingers or a fork. Cut slits in the top crust. Sprinkle the top crust lightly with granulated sugar.

4. Bake 50 to 60 minutes, or until the crust is golden brown and the apples are cooked through (test with a fork). Serve warm with vanilla ice cream, or cold with whipped cream or whipped topping.

Thronis's Blueberry Pie

A FAN OF MEAT pies, Thronis has his favorite sweet pies as well. A giant wearing the right collar cannot lie, so our sources confirm he left out no ingredients. It takes a lot of blueberries to fill a pie for a sky giant. Fortunately, mathematicians have downsized this gigantic recipe to human proportions.

Pie Crust

Use recipe for Grandma Sorenson's Apple Pie (see page 65), or buy 1 (2-count) package prepared pie crusts

¼ cup milk

2 tablespoons sugar

Pie Filling

1¼ cups sugar

5 tablespoons flour

¼ teaspoon cinnamon

Pinch of salt

2 pints of blueberries

1 tablespoon lemon juice

2 tablespoons cold butter, cut into small cubes

1. Preheat the oven to 425 degrees F.

2. Place the first pie crust on the pie pan and trim the edges.

3. Sift the dry ingredients together.

4. Measure ⅓ cup of the dry mixture and spread it across the bottom of the pie shell.

5. Add blueberries, lemon juice, and remaining dry mixture to a bowl and toss together. Pour the blueberry mixture into the pie shell. Place butter cubes over the top of the blueberry mix.

6. Cover with the top shell, trim, seal, and flute. Brush lightly with milk and sprinkle with sugar. Cut a few slits in the top crust.

7. Bake for 50-60 minutes, or until the top is a glossy golden brown.

Olloch the Glutton's Caramel Biscuit Bars

THE NOTORIOUS OLLOCH WILL eat just about anything—he even came to life for a dog biscuit. But *this* biscuit bar is purported to be his favorite. Warning: Do not feed caramel biscuit bars to garden statues, particularly frogs, gargoyles, or gnomes.

1 cup butter, softened

½ cup sugar

½ cup brown sugar

2 egg yolks

¼ teaspoon salt

½ teaspoon baking powder

2¼ cups flour, divided

1–2 cups chocolate chips (Guittard milk chocolate maxi chips or semisweet chips preferred)

20 caramels (Kraft or other brand), unwrapped

1 tablespoon milk

1. Preheat oven to 350 degrees F.

2. Cream together butter, sugars, and egg yolks. Mix dry ingredients then add to the butter and sugar mixture.

3. Spread ¾ of the dough across the bottom of a 9x13 pan. Sprinkle chocolate chips on top.

4. Mix ¼ cup flour into the remaining dough. Crumble across the top of the chocolate chips.

5. Bake for about 20 minutes, or until edges start to turn golden brown. Remove from oven.

6. While the bars are baking, unwrap the caramels and place in small saucepan over low heat. Add a tablespoon of milk and stir until melted and smooth. Drizzle caramel over the top and allow to cool.

7. Once cooled, cut into squares.

Hugo's Mudslide Ice Cream Cake

"HUGO, STOP SINGING," DALE said.

The golem fell silent.

"He isn't very good," Seth said.

"About as musical as a landslide."

—Fablehaven, book 1: *Fablehaven*, p. 155

---

1 batch Viola's Sweetened Whipped
    Cream (see page 60), or
    1 (8-ounce) tub whipped topping

1 (15-ounce) package Oreo cookies
    (42 cookies)

⅓ cup butter, melted

1 (12- to 16-ounce) jar chocolate
    fudge topping

½ (1-gallon) tub ice cream (vanilla or
    chocolate preferred)

1. Make the whipped cream and set aside in refrigerator, or substitute whipped topping.

2. Crush the Oreo cookies and mix with melted butter. Set aside 1½ cups of the cookie mixture for topping. Press the remaining crumb mixture across the bottom of a 9x13 pan. Soften ice cream until spreadable, or cut it and place slices evenly across the crushed cookies. Spread the chocolate fudge topping over the ice cream. Spread whipped cream or whipped topping over fudge topping. Top with the reserved cookie mixture. Freeze until ice cream sets, about 6 hours.

Río Branco Banana Bread with Chocolate Chips

BANANAS ARE PLENTIFUL IN Brazil, home to the Rio Branco preserve. In fact, Brazil is the largest producer of bananas in the Americas. The fairy broker Maddox brought this recipe to Fablehaven after visiting Rio Branco, and Lena sweetened it by adding chocolate chips.

½ cup (1 stick) butter, softened

1 cup sugar

2 eggs

4 very ripe bananas, peeled and mashed

2 cups flour

1 teaspoon baking powder

1 teaspoon baking soda

¼ teaspoon salt

1 cup chocolate chips

1. Cream together butter, sugar, and eggs until well blended. Add bananas and continue to mix. In a separate bowl, combine the flour, baking powder, baking soda, and salt. Slowly add the dry ingredients to the banana mixture, beating on slow speed until incorporated. Fold in chocolate chips.

2. Bake in greased loaf pans at 350 degrees F. for about 60 minutes, or until an inserted toothpick comes out clean.

Grandma Larsen's Sugar Cookies with Cream Cheese Frosting

CHRISTMAS HAD ALWAYS BEEN Kendra's favorite holiday. During her younger years, it had been a day when magic overlapped reality, when the regular routine was suspended and, under the cover of darkness, visitors swooped out of the sky and snuck down the chimney with presents. She had always hoped to stay up late and catch Santa in the act, but she always fell asleep before he came and had to settle for a plate full of cookie crumbs and a thank-you note.

—Fablehaven, book 4: *Secrets of the Dragon Sanctuary*, p. 269

---

2 cups sugar

1 cup (2 sticks) butter, softened

2 eggs

1 tablespoon vanilla

1 cup sour cream

2 teaspoons baking soda

6½ cups flour

1. Preheat oven to 400 degrees F. Cream sugar and butter together until fluffy. Add eggs one at a time, beat until creamy. Add vanilla and sour cream until just mixed. Stir the baking soda into the flour, then slowly add flour mixture to the butter mixture until fully combined. Rest or chill for 30 minutes. Roll out dough on a lightly floured surface. Use cookie cutters to cut out desired shapes. Place on greased or lined cookie sheet. Bake for 8 minutes. Cool on cooling racks, then frost and decorate.

Cream Cheese Frosting

---

1 (8-ounce) package cream cheese, softened

1 cup (2 sticks) butter, softened

4 cups powdered sugar

1-2 teaspoons vanilla

Sprinkles, decorating sugar, or candies for decoration

1. Cream together cream cheese and butter. Beat until light and fluffy. Slowly add powdered sugar and continue to beat. Add vanilla to taste and mix until smooth.

Calico Bread

A ROUND LOAF OF bread sat on the table, a mottled mixture of white, black, brown, and orange. While Lena sliced it, Kendra took another sip of hot chocolate.

"Considering all the ingredients I left out, I thought the brownies might make a jumble pie," Lena said. "But calico loaves are equally delicious. Try a piece."

—Fablehaven, book 1: *Fablehaven*, p. 124

Cinnamon Streusel

⅔ cup brown sugar

½ cup flour

6 tablespoons softened butter

1½ teaspoons cinnamon

Pinch of salt

1. Mix together all of the ingredients with either a pastry blender or a fork. You may need to use your hands to incorporate the butter to form small clumps or crumbles. Set aside the streusel.

You will be making two separate batters to add to the pans.

Banana Bread

1. Make a half batch of Rio Branco Banana Bread on page 71, excluding the chocolate chips.

Chocolate Bread

¼ cup (½ stick) butter	¼ teaspoon salt
¼ cup canola oil	½ teaspoon baking soda
¾ cup sugar	1 teaspoon baking powder
2 eggs	⅔ cup milk
1 cup flour	1 cup chocolate chips
⅓ cup cocoa powder	

1. Preheat oven to 350 degrees F. Grease and flour 2 loaf pans or 1 bundt pan.

2. Cream together the butter, oil, and sugar. Add eggs and continue to beat until mixed thoroughly. In a separate bowl, mix together the flour, cocoa powder, salt, baking soda, and baking powder. Alternate between adding the dry ingredients and the milk to the egg mixture, starting and ending with the dry ingredients. Beat until mixed. Fold in chocolate chips.

1. Using two large spoons or scoops, add the two batters to the pan(s) by alternating scoops of each in a checkerboard pattern.

2. Once all the batter is in the pan(s), sprinkle the cinnamon streusel on top.

3. Bake for approximately 1 hour, or until a toothpick inserted in the center comes out clean.

Vanilla Sauce

⅓ cup milk	2 teaspoons cornstarch
⅓ cup heavy whipping cream	1 tablespoon vanilla
½ cup sugar	

1. While the bread is baking, make the vanilla sauce by combining the milk, cream, and sugar in a saucepan over medium heat. Stir until the sugar dissolves. Add the cornstarch and whisk frequently until the consistency is smooth and there are no lumps. Continue to whisk until the mixture comes to a boil and thickens. Remove from heat and add vanilla. Set aside to cool.

2. Flip the bread onto a cutting board or plate, slice, and serve warm with the vanilla sauce.

Fairy Garden Cupcakes

AFTER LENA AND KENDRA baked and decorated these cupcakes, Kendra took them outside to show the fairies. The tiny winged divas acted disinterested—until Kendra left them on the porch railing and went back inside the house. As soon as the door shut, the cupcakes were swarmed.

Cupcakes

1 (15.25-ounce) box French vanilla cake mix

1 (3.5-ounce) package vanilla instant pudding

¼ cup flour

4 eggs

1 cup sour cream

½ cup canola oil

1 cup water

Buttercream frosting (see recipe on page 61)

Gel food coloring

1 (24-ounce) package fondant (such as Wilton)

1. For cupcakes, line 2–3 pans of standard muffin tins with cupcake liners (to yield 24–30 cupcakes). Preheat oven to 350 degrees F.

2. In a large mixing bowl, add all of the cupcake ingredients. Beat on low speed until moistened. Beat on medium speed for about 2 minutes, scraping sides of bowl as necessary.

3. Pour batter into lined tins, filling ½ to ⅔ full. Bake for about 15 minutes, or until a toothpick inserted in the center comes out clean. Remove cupcakes from oven and cool completely on cooling rack.

4. To decorate the cupcakes, use a 1M (open star) piping tip to make simple flowers in the colors of your choosing. Use a leaf tip to add leaves. Use a rolling pin to roll out a golf ball–sized chunk of fondant in a thin, even layer. Use a small heart-shaped cookie cutter to cut out heart shapes. Place hearts in pairs with the tips down into the frosting flowers (to look like fairy wings).

Dragon Egg Cupcakes

MOTHER DRAGONS DILIGENTLY PROTECT their clutches of eggs. Daring collectors have tried to smuggle dragon eggs off sanctuaries, but their attempts tend to prove fatal. If you wish to simulate the experience of dining on dragon eggs without losing your life, these dragon egg cupcakes should fill the need.

1 (15.25-ounce) package devil's food cake mix

1 (3.5-ounce) package chocolate instant pudding

¼ cup flour

4 eggs

1 cup sour cream

½ cup canola oil

1 cup water

1½ cups chocolate chips

Buttercream frosting (see recipe on page 61)

1 cup sweetened shredded coconut, toasted

1 (7-ounce) package speckled jelly bird egg candies or Cadbury mini egg candies

1. For cupcakes, line standard muffin tins with cupcake liners (24–30). Preheat oven to 350 degrees F.

2. In a large mixing bowl, add all of the cupcake ingredients except the chocolate chips. Beat on low speed until moistened. Beat on medium speed for about 2 minutes, scraping sides of bowl as necessary. Fold in chocolate chips.

3. Pour batter into lined tins, filling ½ to ⅔ full. Bake for about 15 minutes, or until a toothpick inserted in the center comes out clean. Remove cupcakes from oven and cool completely on cooling rack.

4. To toast coconut, place it in a medium-size nonstick frying pan. Heat over medium heat, stirring constantly until golden brown. Immediately remove from heat and transfer to a plate or cookie sheet to cool.

5. To decorate cupcakes, pipe a rim around the top of the cupcake using a size 10 or larger (round) piping tip. Fill the inside of the rim with toasted coconut. Place 2–3 egg candies on top.

S'MORES PIZZA

GAVIN LIKES TO EAT all sorts of things, including this delicious treat.

AFTER THE MEAL, THEY broke out graham crackers, chocolate bars, and marshmallows to make gooey s'mores. Gavin and Tanu let their marshmallows catch fire and ate them charred, but Kendra preferred to patiently roast hers to a golden brown.

—Fablehaven, book 4: *Secrets of the Dragon Sanctuary*, p. 344

1 (13.8-ounce) package refrigerated pizza dough (such as Pillsbury)

1 cup (about 8 full sheets) graham cracker crumbs

2 tablespoons sugar

6 tablespoons melted butter

¼ teaspoon sea salt

⅓ cup biscoff cookie butter

1 cup chocolate chips

1 cup mini marshmallows

1. Cook pizza dough according to package directions (8–10 minutes at 350 degrees F.). Leave oven at 350 degrees F.

2. Prepare graham cracker crumble by breaking full sheets of graham crackers in half and placing in a food processor and grinding until they are fine crumbs. Stir in sugar, melted butter, and sea salt until fully mixed.

3. Spread biscoff cookie butter over entire crust, leaving ½ inch around all edges. Sprinkle chocolate chips over cookie butter, spread evenly over the entire pizza. Repeat with the marshmallows. Crumble the graham cracker mixture over the top of the marshmallows and chocolate chips. Bake until marshmallows start to puff and turn golden brown, approximately 3 minutes.

4. Remove from oven and cut into square or triangular slices to serve.

Garus's Wild Brownies

EVEN THE WILD BROWNIES at Fablehaven take great pride in having a dessert named after them. Be careful—this recipe from Garus might tempt you to kidnap some brownies of your own.

Nonstick cooking spray

¾ cup sugar

¾ cup light brown sugar

5 tablespoons butter, melted

2 large eggs

¼ cup canola oil

2 tablespoons water

2 teaspoons vanilla

¾ cup flour

⅔ cup cocoa powder

½ cup powdered sugar

¾ cup chocolate chips

¾ teaspoon salt

1. Preheat oven to 325 degrees F. Lightly spray an 8x8 pan with cooking spray and line with parchment paper.

2. In a large bowl, mix the sugars and the melted butter. In a separate bowl, whisk together the eggs, oil, water, and vanilla, then add to the sugar mix. In a dry bowl, mix flour, cocoa powder, powdered sugar, chocolate chips, and salt. Stir the dry mixture into the wet mixture until just combined.

3. Pour the batter into the prepared pan and smooth it out to form an even layer. Bake for about 44 minutes, or until a toothpick comes out with a few crumbs on it (not wet). Cool pan on a cooling rack, then slice into squares.

To Make Brownie Footprints

1. Create a stencil using parchment, copy, or construction paper. Trace, draw, or print small footprints or shoe prints on the paper. Cut out the small footprints, keeping the paper around the print intact.

2. Place the template over a brownie square, and sift powdered sugar over the top using a sifter or fine mesh sieve. Remove the paper from the brownie to reveal tiny footprints.

Goblin Glop Trifle

IF YOU EVER NEED a favor from the goblins who work in the dungeon at Fablehaven, this trifle is your ticket—perhaps because the chocolate mousse looks like glop. But don't serve it to a goblin on a plate. Instead, put several spoonfuls in a blender and then serve it like a soup.

---

2 batches of brownies (see Garus's Wild Brownies recipe on page 83 or make your favorite boxed mix)

1 (5.1-ounce) package chocolate instant pudding

1½ cups milk

1 (8-ounce) package cream cheese, softened

2 double batches of Viola's Sweetened Whipped Cream, or 2 (12-ounce) tubs whipped topping, divided

1 bar of high quality chocolate, shaved

1. Follow box instructions to make a double batch of your favorite brownie recipe and allow to cool completely. Cut brownies into small (½- to 1-inch) cubes. Save crumbs for trifle topping.

2. To make chocolate mousse, begin by making a double batch of Viola's Sweetened Whipped Cream (skip this step if using whipped topping). Set aside.

3. Whisk together milk and pudding mix. Let sit for a few minutes. Add cream cheese and beat together until smooth.

4. Fold the whipped cream or whipped topping into the pudding mixture. Refrigerate until ready to assemble trifle.

5. Make another double batch of Viola's Sweetened Whipped Cream (skip this step if using whipped topping) and refrigerate until ready to assemble trifle.

6. To assemble trifle, begin by loosely layering approximately half the brownie cubes at the bottom of the trifle dish. Next, spread half of the chocolate mousse over the top of the brownies. Layer half of the whipped cream on top of the mousse and spread evenly. Repeat the 3 layers one more time. Sprinkle the brownie crumbs and shaved chocolate on top of the final layer of whipped cream. Refrigerate trifle until ready to serve.

 If you have a small trifle dish or clear bowl instead of a large trifle dish, this recipe can be cut in half.

Oozing Tar Cakes

THESE GOOEY CONFECTIONS ARE the perfect dessert for fiftieth birthday parties, gothic bridal showers, Wednesday Addams's quinceañera, or celebrating the death of a demon. Because nothing says congratulations better than cakes that ooze dark chocolate.

½ cup (1 stick) unsalted butter

6 ounces bittersweet chocolate, chopped into bits

2 large eggs plus 2 large egg yolks

¼ cup sugar

⅛ teaspoon salt

3 tablespoons flour

Powdered sugar or other toppings

1. Preheat oven to 450 degrees F. Lightly grease and flour 4 large (6-ounce) or 6 small (4-ounce) ramekins. Tap out excess flour and place ramekins on a baking sheet. Add butter and chocolate to a double boiler over low heat and melt until smooth, or add butter and chocolate to a microwave-safe bowl and heat for 30 second increments, stirring in between. Melt and stir until smooth.

2. In a separate bowl, combine the eggs, egg yolks, sugar, and salt. Beat the mixture until thick and creamy and color lightens.

3. Fold the melted chocolate and the flour into the egg mixture.

4. Pour the batter into the prepared ramekins.

5. Bake for about 8 to 10 minutes, or until the sides of the cakes are set, but the center is still soft. Cool the cakes in the ramekins for 2 minutes. One by one, place a small plate over the top of a ramekin and carefully flip the cake onto the plate. Wait about 10 seconds, then remove the ramekin. Top cakes with sifted powdered sugar or other toppings, and serve immediately.

Kendra's Chocolate-Covered Krispies

ONE STORMY NIGHT, KENDRA placed a few of her favorite things on the kitchen counter for the brownies: Cocoa Krispies cereal, chocolate chips, and peanut butter. After a tedious stretch in the attic listening to thunder rattle the shingles, she awoke the next morning to find this crunchy treat waiting for her.

Butter, shortening, or nonstick baking spray

6 cups toasted puffed rice cereal, such as Rice Krispies or Cocoa Krispies

1 cup creamy peanut butter

1 cup sugar

1 cup light corn syrup

2 cups milk chocolate chips (or semisweet if preferred)

1. Grease a 9x13 pan.

2. Pour cereal into a large bowl. In a medium saucepan, add peanut butter, sugar, and corn syrup. Bring to a boil, stirring constantly.

3. Pour the hot peanut butter mixture over the cereal and mix well. Pour the mixture into the greased 9x13 pan and spread evenly, pressing down gently.

4. Melt chocolate chips in a microwave-safe bowl. Heat in 30-second increments, stirring between, until smooth.

5. Pour the melted chocolate over the cereal mixture in the pan and spread into an even layer. Allow to cool and set before cutting and serving.

Fairy in a Jar
Layered Gelatin Treats

FAIRY BROKERS CAPTURE AND trade fairies for a living. This recipe was discovered by Grandpa while attending the Fairy Brokers Convention in 2006. Though this dessert was all the rage among attendees, some outspoken fairy activists have complained it looks like imps waiting to happen. We'll let you be the judge.

Graham Cracker Crust

Nonstick cooking spray

1½ cups (about 12 full sheets) graham cracker crumbs

½ cup butter, melted

3 tablespoons sugar

Cheesecake Layer

1 (8-ounce) package cream cheese, softened

1 cup sugar

1 teaspoon vanilla

1 (8-ounce) tub whipped topping or 1 batch of Viola's Sweetened Whipped Cream (see recipe on page 60)

Raspberry Gelatin Layer

2 cups boiling water

1 (6-ounce) package raspberry gelatin, such as Jell-O

1 (16-ounce) bag frozen raspberries

1 (6-ounce) bag gummy candy worms, dragonflies, butterflies, or other creatures

1. Preheat oven to 350 degrees F. Lightly grease a 9x13 pan with cooking spray. Breaking the graham crackers in half or fourths first, crush them in a blender or food processor until they are fine crumbs. Melt butter and let cool slightly. In a large bowl, combine graham cracker crumbs, butter, and sugar until well mixed. Press mixture onto the bottom of the pan. Bake for 8–10 minutes. Let cool completely.

2. For the cheesecake filling, beat cream cheese in a mixing bowl until light and fluffy (about 2 minutes). Add the sugar and vanilla. Continue to beat until well mixed. Fold in the whipped topping or whipped cream.

3. Divide the filling into 8 mason jars and spread evenly across the bottoms of the jars. Place jars in the refrigerator while preparing the gelatin layer.

4. For gelatin layer, empty gelatin mix into a bowl, then add boiling water. Whisk well until combined. Pour in the bag of frozen raspberries and stir. Pour the gelatin mixture on top of the cheesecake filling mixture in the jars. Place jars back in refrigerator to cool and set. After about 10 minutes—once gelatin layer is no longer hot but not yet set—place one gummy candy* in each jar, pushing candy into the gelatin layer against the side of the jar. Place back in refrigerator to cool and set completely.

5. Break up graham cracker crust from 9x13 pan and crumble over the gelatin layer in the jars. If desired, add more whipped cream as a topping.

6. Alternatively, this dessert may be prepared in a 9x13 pan. If preparing in a 9x13 pan, layer the cheesecake filling over the cooled graham crust, then layer the gelatin over the cheesecake layer. Add gummy candies around the edges of the pan.

 If desired, you can make your own fairies by melting chocolate in candy molds to use in place of the gummy candies.

DRINKS

SETH WAS HERE

Dale's Fairy Milk

KENDRA EYED THE TIN of milk. Drink the milk. She dipped a finger and put it in her mouth. It was sweet and warm. For an instant the sun gleamed in her eyes, making her blink.

She glanced back at her brother, who was creeping up on a small group of hovering fairies. Three had wings like butterflies, one like a dragonfly. She could not suppress a shriek at the impossible sight.

Kendra looked back at the milk. A fairy with hummingbird wings was drinking from her cupped hand.

—Fablehaven, book 1: *Fablehaven*, p. 73

---

1 cup milk

1 teaspoon sugar (or other sweetener of choice)

¼ teaspoon vanilla

Gel food coloring

1. Combine milk, sweetener, and vanilla. Stir until sweetener dissolves. Add a small amount of gel food coloring and stir. Enjoy! Can be served hot or cold.

Shadow Charmer's Hot Chocolate Draught

SEARCHING CLAMMY CATACOMBS FOR wraiths and liches can be icy work. This bracing beverage will warm you against the magical fear generated by the undead, or simply cheer you up on a frosty evening. One sip and you will never venture into a subterranean crypt without it.

1 (8-ounce) package semi-sweet chocolate, chopped, or 1 (8-ounce) bag high-quality semi-sweet chocolate chips (such as Guittard Super Cookie Chips)

2 cups milk (2% or whole preferred)

2 cups half-and-half

¼ teaspoon cinnamon, divided

Viola's Sweetened Whipped Cream (see recipe on page 60) or whipped topping, marshmallows, and chocolate sprinkles for topping, if desired

Cinnamon sticks for garnish, if desired

1. Place all ingredients except the cinnamon in a medium saucepan and whisk over medium heat until hot. Mix in 1/8 teaspoon cinnamon. Remove from heat.

2. Pour into mugs or glasses and top with whipped cream, marshmallows, and sprinkles. Dust each hot chocolate with a pinch of the remaining cinnamon. Add one or two cinnamon sticks for garnish, if desired.

TANU'S BOTTLED-UP EMOTIONS

TANU'S FAMILY HAS LONG protected the recipe for potions capable of altering human feelings. Since magical ingredients like dragon tears are needed for these elixirs to take full effect, the potion master has shared flavorful imitations of his signature concoctions. Who doesn't have a little more courage with the taste of raspberries on their lips?

Several (12.7-ounce) bottles flavored syrups (such as Torani)

Crushed ice

1 (1-pint) container heavy whipping cream or half-and-half

1 (2-liter) bottle club soda

1 batch Viola's Sweetened Whipped Cream (see recipe on page 60) or 1 (8-ounce) tub whipped topping, maraschino cherries or other fruit for toppings

1. Using a large clear (12- to 16-ounce) cup or glass, pour in any combination of flavored syrups, 1 to 2 tablespoons total. Some popular combos are mango and peach, raspberry and vanilla, or pineapple and coconut.

2. Add ½ cup ice and 1 tablespoon heavy cream or half-and-half. Next, slowly pour in 8 ounces of club soda, stirring gently once full.

3. Top with whipped cream and a cherry or other fruit.

Singing Sisters Bubbling Brew

THOSE WHO SING IN the kitchen will find it natural to brew this beverage. While making this punch and staring into the swirling dry ice, you may glimpse the image of a forthcoming dragon storm. If you do, please alert your local chapter of the Knights of the Dawn.

1 (48-ounce) can pineapple juice

1 cup lemonade or pink lemonade

1 (2-liter) bottle of lemon-lime soda (such as Sprite)

1 (0.16-ounce) package tropical punch or other colorful unsweetened powdered drink mix

Ice

Dry ice

1. Mix pineapple juice, lemonade, and soda together in a large pitcher or drink dispenser. Add ice. Sprinkle with powdered drink mix, allowing color to slowly disperse instead of stirring it in. Before serving, add a small chunk of dry ice for fog effect.

Savani's Tropical Smoothie

THE CRESCENT LAGOON DRAGON sanctuary hosts many species of magical creatures found on few other preserves. The caretaker Savani delights the local menehune with this refreshing blend of island flavors.

"WELCOME TO CRESCENT LAGOON," she said. "I am Savani. This is the hallowed island of Timbuli."

—Dragonwatch, book 3: *Master of the Phantom Isle*, p. 190

¾ cup pineapple juice

½ cup canned coconut milk

1 large frozen banana, peeled

1 cup frozen mango chunks

1 cup frozen strawberries

½ cup ice

1 teaspoon honey

1. Add ingredients to blender and blend until smooth and creamy. Pour into cups and enjoy!

BRANDON'S FAVORITES

SETH WAS HERE

ECLAIRS

Pastry Shells

½ cup (1 stick) butter

1 cup water

1 cup all-purpose flour

¼ teaspoon salt

4 eggs

1. Preheat oven to 450 degrees F. Grease or line a cookie sheet with parchment paper.

2. In a medium saucepan, combine butter and water. Bring to a boil, stirring until butter melts completely. Reduce heat to low and add flour and salt. Stir well until the mixture leaves the sides of the pan and begins to form a stiff ball. Remove from heat. Add eggs one at a time, beating well to incorporate completely.

3. Prepare a pastry bag with a No. 10 tip or larger; or, cut one corner of a gallon size zip-top bag to make a 1-inch hole. Fill the bag with pastry dough and pipe onto cookie sheet in approximately 1½-inch x 4-inch strips.

4. Bake 15 minutes in the preheated oven, then reduce the heat to 325 degrees F. and bake 20 minutes more. Pastries should be a pale golden brown and sound hollow when lightly tapped on bottom. Cool completely on a wire rack.

Cream Filling

1½ cups heavy cream

⅓ cup powdered sugar

1 teaspoon vanilla

1 (5-ounce) package instant vanilla pudding mix

2½ cups cold milk

1. Beat the cream, powdered sugar, and vanilla on high speed until stiff peaks form. Set whipped cream aside. In a separate bowl, combine the pudding mix and milk. Whisk for 1–2 minutes, then place in refrigerator for 5–10 minutes to softly set. Once the pudding is softly set, gently fold the whipped cream into the pudding.

2. Carefully cut the tops off of the cooled pastry shells with a serrated knife. Fill shells with the pudding mixture and replace tops.

Ganache Topping

1 (12-ounce) package high quality semisweet chocolate chips

1½ cups heavy cream

1. Place the chocolate in a medium bowl. Heat the cream in a small saucepan over medium heat or in the microwave in 1-minute increments. Bring just to a boil, watching carefully to remove from the heat as soon as it begins to boil. Pour the hot cream over the chocolate and let sit for a few minutes, then whisk until smooth. Using a spoon or piping bag, spread generously over the top of the eclairs.

2. Place eclairs in the refrigerator to cool and set for a few hours before serving.

Key Lime Pie

Graham Cracker Crust

1½ cups (about 12 full sheets) graham cracker crumbs

6 tablespoons melted butter

⅓ cup sugar

¼ teaspoon sea salt

1. Preheat the oven to 350 degrees F.

2. Breaking the graham cracker sheets into halves or fourths, process them in a blender or food processor until they are fine crumbs. Mix the graham cracker crumbs, melted butter, sugar, and salt in a medium bowl until combined.

3. Press into the bottom of a 9-inch pie pan or springform pan, pushing along bottom and sides to create an even layer. Bake for 6–7 minutes. Remove from oven and cool.

Filling

6 egg yolks

1 tablespoon finely grated key lime zest

1½ (14-ounce) cans sweetened condensed milk

¾ cup fresh squeezed key lime juice (the juice of approximately 18 key limes, can substitute Nellie and Joe's bottled key lime juice if preferred)

1 batch Viola's Sweetened Whipped Cream (see recipe on page 60), or 1 (12-ounce) tub whipped topping

½ (4-ounce) bar white chocolate, roughly grated

1. While crust is cooling, whisk together the egg yolks and lime zest until well mixed, about 1 minute. Add the condensed milk and lime juice, whisking after each addition. Pour into the graham cracker crust.

2. Bake until filling is firm in the middle, about 15–20 minutes. Remove from oven and cool on wire rack. Once cooled, refrigerate until cold and firm, at least a few hours.

3. Make a batch of Viola's Sweetened Whipped Cream, or use 1 tub whipped topping. Use a piping bag to pipe swirls or rosettes all along the edge of the pie, or cover the top of the pie completely with whipped cream and spread evenly. Sprinkle it with white chocolate gratings. Chill until ready to serve.

Chessmen Banana Pudding Dessert

2 (7.25-ounce) bags Pepperidge
  Farm Chessmen butter cookies

7 bananas, sliced

2 cups milk

1 (5-ounce) box instant vanilla
  pudding

1 (8-ounce) package cream cheese,
  softened

1 (14-ounce) can sweetened
  condensed milk

1½ batches of Viola's Sweetened
  Whipped Cream (see recipe on
  page 60) or 1 (12-ounce) tub
  whipped topping

1. Line the bottom of a 9x13 pan with one bag of the cookies. Layer the sliced bananas on top of the cookies.

2. In a bowl, combine milk and pudding mix. Whisk well.

3. In a separate bowl, combine the cream cheese and condensed milk. Blend until smooth.

4. Fold the whipped cream (or whipped topping) into the cream cheese mixture.

5. Add the cream cheese mixture to the pudding mixture, and stir until fully mixed. Pour the mixture over the bananas and cookies.

6. Cover with the second bag of cookies. Refrigerate until ready to serve.

CRAFTS

SETH WAS HERE

Shapeshifter Play Dough

SOME OF THE CREATURES at the magical preserves are constructed from natural elements and later brought to life. Examples include golems, dullions, and the nimble limberjack, Mendigo.

> "WHAT'S THE DIFFERENCE BETWEEN a dullion and a golem?"
>
> "Quality, mostly," Vanessa said. "Dullions are a bit easier to create. Although I haven't seen one in ages. Like golems, they're nearly extinct."
>
> —Fablehaven, book 2: *Rise of the Evening Star*, p. 74

1 cup flour

⅓ cup salt

1 tablespoon cream of tartar

1 tablespoon oil

¾ to 1 cup boiling water

Food coloring

1. Mix dry ingredients in a large bowl. Add the oil and stir. Carefully pour in the hot water. Mix together until a dough is formed. Let dough cool, then divide into sections and add a small amount of food coloring. Knead dough until coloring is uniform. Store in airtight containers.

CRAFTS

HUGO'S KINETIC SAND

NOBODY CAN MANIPULATE SAND and soil like an earth golem. Hugo whipped up this simple formula for humans who want sand they can shape.

> THE HERCULEAN MOWER TURNED and jogged toward them with long, loping strides. Seth could feel the ground vibrate as Hugo approached. Still clutching the scythes, the massive golem came to a halt in front of Dale, looming over him.
>
> "He's made of dirt?" Seth asked.
>
> "Soil, clay, and stone," Dale said. "Granted the semblance of life by a powerful enchanter. Hugo was donated to the preserve a couple hundred years ago."
>
> —Fablehaven, book 1: *Fablehaven*, p. 154

2 cups fine sand

1 cup cornstarch

⅓ cup oil

A few drops of food coloring (optional)

1–2 tablespoons liquid dish soap

1. Mix sand and cornstarch together. Add oil and mix well. If using food coloring, add along with the oil. Mix in liquid dish soap 1 tablespoon at a time until desired texture is reached.

Vanessa's Invisible Ink

IN A PINCH, SENDING secret messages can be incredibly handy. Vanessa has several techniques for passing information while avoiding detection.

Lemon Juice Method

Juice of ½ a lemon
A few drops of water

1. Mix the lemon juice and a few drops of water in a bowl. Dip a cotton swab or paintbrush in the lemon juice and write your message on a piece of white paper. Allow the invisible ink to dry. Once dry, hold the paper with the message over a hot lightbulb or a lit candle until the message reappears. If using a candle, have an adult supervise, and be careful to not place the paper too close to the flame.

Baking Soda Method

¼ cup baking soda
¼ cup water

Dark-colored juice, such as concord grape juice

1. Mix the baking soda and water in a bowl. Dip a cotton swab or paintbrush in the baking soda solution and write your message on a piece of white paper. Allow the invisible ink to dry. Dip a paintbrush into the grape juice and paint the juice over the message. The message will reappear.

Milk Method

½ cup milk
Lightbulb or candle

1. To use the milk method, dip a cotton swab or paintbrush into the milk and write your message on a piece of white paper. Allow the milk to dry for about 30 minutes. Expose the message to heat with a lightbulb, candle, or iron. If using a candle, have an adult supervise, and be careful to not place the paper too close to the flame. As the paper heats up, the message will reappear.

WIZARD SLIME

NUMEROUS ADVENTURERS HAVE PERISHED in the bowels of a necropolis or the heart of a fetid swamp only to have their remains disintegrated by a mass of carnivorous slime. But what if that slime could be tamed? Stretch it, squeeze it, bounce it, poke it, flatten it, roll it—the possibilities are many.

> KENDRA REACHED INTO THE sack and then sprinkled raisins into the glass cylinder. The orange mass at the bottom oozed toward the raisins like living pudding, covering them and slowly darkening to a deep red. "You have gross pets," Kendra said.
>
> Vanessa lifted her gaze from the journal she was studying. "Wizard slime looks unappetizing, but no other substance can equal its ability to draw out the poison from infected tissue. All of my darlings have their uses."
>
> —Fablehaven, book 2: *Rise of the Evening Star*, p. 190

⅔ cup water-soluble school glue, such as Elmer's

¼ cup water

½ teaspoon baking soda

2½ cups shaving cream, such as Barbasol or Gillette

Liquid food coloring

1½ tablespoons contact lens solution (containing boric acid and sodium borate), such as Bausch + Lomb Biotrue or Acuvue

1. Pour the glue into a bowl. Add water and baking soda, stir.
2. Add shaving cream and mix. For fluffier slime, add more shaving cream.
3. Add food coloring and mix.
4. Slowly add the contact lens solution, and knead the slime. It will be sticky.
5. Add more contact lens solution or a little baby oil if it gets too sticky to knead.

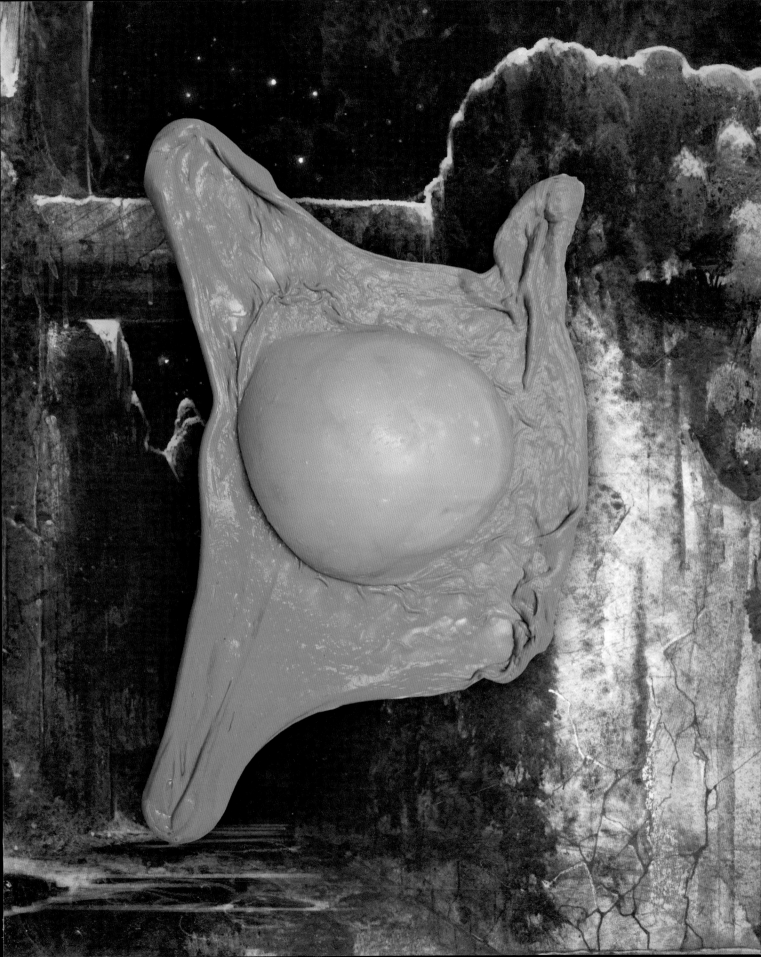

Tanu's Giant Bubble Solution

TANU IS A POTION master with many hidden talents. His creations can increase or decrease size, summon potent emotions, and even morph the drinker into a gaseous state. When Grandpa wants to give the fairies of Fablehaven bubbles to play with, Tanu has a perfect solution in his arsenal.

Bubble Wand

2 plastic drinking straws
1 (approx. 5-foot-long) strand yarn

1. Thread the yarn through both straws and tie a knot in the yarn to close the loop. Trim the ends or hide knot in one straw. Separate straws so that they are opposite each other on the yarn loop.

Bubble Solution

1 cup water   2 tablespoons glycerin
2 tablespoons Dawn dish soap

1. Place all ingredients in a bowl and stir slowly. Let sit for at least an hour, or even for a day if you plan ahead. Pour into a large, shallow baking dish or aluminum roasting pan. Holding one straw in each hand, fully submerge bubble wand in the solution, then raise up and out, slowly waving through the air to make bubbles. It may take a few tries to get a bubble going.

INDEX

ABOUT THE AUTHORS

BRANDON MULL is the #1 *New York Times* best-selling author of the Fablehaven, Candy Shop War, Beyonders, and Five Kingdoms series. A kinetic thinker, Brandon enjoys bouncy balls, squeezable stress toys, and popping bubble wrap. He lives in Utah in a happy little valley near the mouth of a canyon with his wife, Erlyn, their eleven children, and some animals. Brandon loves meeting his readers and hearing about their experiences with his books.

CHERIE MULL is a mom of four who has always loved making and eating good food. After graduating with a degree in biology, Cherie worked in gene sequencing and pharmaceutical research before exchanging her lab coat for an apron. She now owns a thriving baking business, creating cakes and custom treats for weddings, birthdays, and other celebrations. Cherie and her husband, Bryson—Brandon Mull's brother—have been beta readers for the Fablehaven stories since the beginning, and she is thrilled to be a part of this new adventure.